Copyright © 2015 by Coren Jonathan Allen & Francesca Da Sacco

ISBN: 978-0-9964050-1-0

All rights reserved. No literal or illustrative part of this book may be used or reproduced in any manner whatsoever without written permission from the author.

The author & illustrator retain sole copyright to the contents and illustrations in this book.

FIRST EDITION

The MESSAGE of this book should be duplicated and reproduced everywhere and as often as possible.

Education powers thought.
Thoughts generate action.
Actions fuel the planet...for better or for worse.

1 2 3 4 5 6

Etihad Airways is pleased to print this book in honor of the 2019 Year of Tolerance.

Tolerance is a virtue and an intrinsic part of the Islamic culture. It is observed at all levels: individual, organizational and national. With more than 200 nationalities living peacefully and successfully in the United Arab Emirates (UAE), the UAE society has been an undisputed example of being a tolerant and inclusive country.

Saeed Alsuwaidi is an Emirati Citizen and a champion for the education of peace and tolerance in schools. A UAE expert, he clearly articulates the vision of the UAE and the 2019 Year of Tolerance. Saeed is a graduate student at the internationally renowned School for Conflict Analysis & Resolution at George Mason University in Northern Virginia.

What if it Just Started Raining?

YEAR OF TOLERANCE

On 15 December 2018, H. H. Sheikh Khalifa bin Zayed declared 2019 as the Year of Tolerance. The announcement aims to highlight the UAE as a global capital for tolerance and its approach, since its establishment, to be a bridge of communication between peoples of different cultures in a respectful environment that rejects extremism and emphasizes on the acceptance of the other.

"In our zeal just to survive or succeed, we forget
that life is better when we are good to each other.

As rain replenishes the earth, and thus the body...smiles
replenish the soul, kindness & generosity replenish
the heart, and forgiveness replenishes the mind."
(Coren Jonathan Allen)

For Isabella & Gabriella

What if it just started raining?

"Papa, the earth is dry and we have no food. The village is starving. What are we going to do?"

Papa closes his eyes, turns his head to the sky and asks...

"What if it just started raining?"

"Does the rain stay away because we have dark skin Papa?"

"No my son, the rain does not care what color your skin is."

"Is it because of our name or the language we speak?"

"No my son, the rain does not care what your name is, who your parents are or the language you speak. Rain is for everyone."

"Now, we must pray for rain to come so the people can be refreshed."

During the night, the rain comes...

And the earth is no longer dry.

Flowers bloom.

Crops grow.

Color returns to the earth and health to the people because they have food to eat and fresh water to drink which keeps them strong and healthy.

"Papa, the spirit of the people is dry. Their souls are starving. What are we going to do?"

Papa closes his eyes, turns his head to the sky and asks...

"What if it just started raining smiles?"

"Do smiles stay away because we have dark skin Papa?"

"No my son, a smile does not care what color your skin is."

"Is it because of our name or the language we speak?"

"No my son, a smile does not care what your name is, who your parents are or the language you speak. Smiles are for everyone."

"Now, we must pray for smiles to come so the spirit of the people can be refreshed."

During the night, the rain comes...

And the village people begin to smile at one another and to visiting strangers from faraway lands.

The spirit of the village is no longer dry.

Relationships bloom.

Hearts grow.

Color returns to the soul of the village.

KINDNESS & GENEROSITY (heart)

"Papa, the heart of the people is dry. They are sad. What are we going to do?"

Papa closes his eyes, turns his head to the sky and asks...

"What if it just started raining kindness and generosity?"

"Do kindness and generosity stay away because we have dark skin Papa?"

"No my son, a kind deed does not care what color your skin is."

"Is it because of our name or the language we speak?"

"No my son, a generous spirit does not care what your name is, who your parents are or the language you speak. Kindness and generosity are for everyone."

"Now, we must pray for kindness and generosity to come so the heart of the people can be refreshed."

During the night, the rain comes...

And the village people begin to show kindness to each other. They share their food and belongings, and show hospitality to visiting strangers from faraway lands.

The heart of the village is no longer dry.

Kindness blooms.

Generosity grows.

Color returns to the heart of the village.

"Papa, the mind of the people is dry. They are angry at each other. What are we going to do?"

Papa closes his eyes, turns his head to the sky and asks...

"What if it just started raining forgiveness?"

"Does forgiveness stay away because we have dark skin Papa?"

"No my son, forgiveness does not care what color your skin is."

"Is it because of our name or the language we speak?"

"No my son, a forgiving spirit does not care what your name is, who your parents are or the language you speak. Forgiveness is for everyone."

"Now, we must pray for the villagers to forgive each other so the mind of the people can be refreshed."

During the night, the rain comes...

And the village people begin to forgive each other. They forgive the mistakes of their neighbors and also those of strangers from faraway lands... because they also want forgiveness in return for their own mistakes.

The mind of the village is no longer dry.

Forgiveness blooms.

Tolerance and acceptance grows.

Color returns to the mind of the people.

"You see my son, when the soul, heart and mind of the people are dry, you can make it rain whenever you wish.

Rain does not care what color your skin is or in which village you were born.

Rain does not care what tribe you are from or what language you speak.

Rain does not care if you are a boy or a girl...if you are big or small...fast or slow...old or young.

Rain is for everyone and makes us all better people.

For we are one people even though we live in many villages.

While humanity may indeed have many differences of color, language, size, gender and origin, we know that there is only one human race. Do not forget that the rain is for all of us.

Life is better when it rains smiles...even when you don't feel like smiling.

Life is better when it rains kindness and generosity…even when others refuse to be kind or share.

Life is better when it rains forgiveness…even when others refuse to forgive.

And the best thing of all…the rain is free. It does not cost us anything to be good to each other.

My son, there will always be times when the people forget that life is better when it rains, and they just need a reminder.

Show them smiles, kindness, generosity and forgiveness.

And by doing so, you will make it rain wherever you are."

Hypothesis:

"Aesop (Aesop's Fables) and Dr. Seuss wrote children's stories with messages meant for adults.

We teach our children and read to them with fervor but often neglect to apply what we want them to learn in our own daily living.

We forget the lessons when we grow up.

In our zeal just to survive or succeed, we forget that life is better when we are good to each other."

(Coren Jonathan Allen)

Coren Jonathan Allen in Caorle, Italy, 2015

Francesca Da Sacco in Padua, Italy

Author

Coren Jonathan Allen is a retired US Army Soldier, author & aspiring entrepreneur. As founder of The Kambimbi Academy (based on this book) Coren seeks to spark an international movement that will generate a positive shift in social norms. He believes that Hate is a Contagion of the soul and intends to combat Hate through educational immunology--and further, drive this initiative to policy. In so doing he will bring a message of enduring Hope to the entire planet. Coren has travelled and worked in more than 29 countries on 5 continents.

Illustrator

Francesca Da Sacco is an Italian comic artist, writer and illustrator. She created her first comic book at age 11 and since then she hasn't stopped drawing. Since 2002 she has written for multiple Italian publishers and illustrated 2 graphic novels. Francesca continues to work as a freelance artist illustrating children's books, e-books and APPS. Much of her work can be found at: http://francescadasacco.wix.com/artwork.